FOR BY HIM WERE ALL THINGS CREATED

Charlcia Bright

WestBow Press books may be ordered through booksellers or by contacting:

WestBow Press
A Division of Thomas Nelson & Zondervan
1663 Liberty Drive
Bloomington, IN 47403
www.westbowpress.com
844-714-3454

Because of the dynamic nature of the Internet, any web addresses or links contained in this book may have changed since publication and may no longer be valid. The views expressed in this work are solely those of the author and do not necessarily reflect the views of the publisher, and the publisher hereby disclaims any responsibility for them.

Any people depicted in stock imagery provided by Getty Images are models, and such images are being used for illustrative purposes only.
Certain stock imagery © Getty Images.

All Scripture quotations are taken from the King James Version.

ISBN: 978-1-6642-3588-5 (sc)
ISBN: 978-1-6642-3589-2 (e)

Library of Congress Control Number: 2021910906

Print information available on the last page.

WestBow Press rev. date: 06/25/2021

WestBow
PRESS®
A DIVISION OF THOMAS NELSON
& ZONDERVAN

Psalm 90:2 Before the mountains were brought forth, or ever Thou hadst formed the earth and the world, even from everlasting to everlasting, Thou art God.

Isaiah 40:8 The grass withereth, the flower faded: but the word of our God shall stand forever.

Exodus 3:14 And God said unto Moses, I AM THAT I AM.

Isaiah 55:9 For as the heavens are higher than the earth, so are my ways higher than your ways, and my thoughts than your thoughts.

Ecclesiastes 3:1 To every thing there is a season, and a time to every purpose under heaven.

Proverbs 3:6 In all thy ways acknowledge him, and he shall direct thy paths.

Job 12:7 But ask now the beasts, and they shall teach; and the fowls of the air, and they shall tell thee.

Romans 10:13 Whosoever shall call upon the name of the Lord shall be saved.

Photo: Charlcia Bright   Artwork: Tristan Ellis

Isaiah 41:10 Fear thou not; for I am with thee: be not dismayed; for I am thy God.

Job 12:10 In whose hand is the soul of every living thing, and the breadth of all mankind.

John 10:10 I am come that they might have life, and that they might have it more abundantly.

2 Corinthians 5:17 Therefore if any man be in Christ, he is a new creature:
old things are passed away; behold, all things are new.

2 Corinthians 12:9 And he said unto me, my grace is sufficient for thee: for my strength is made perfect in weakness.

Psalm 33:5 He loveth righteousness and judgement: the earth is full of the goodness of the Lord.

John 14:1 Let not your heart be troubled: ye believe in God, believe also in me.

Photo: Charlcia Bright   Heart: Hannah Ramsey

Psalm 85:11 Truth shall spring out of the earth; and righteousness shall look down from heaven.

Psalm 86:9 All nations whom thou hast made shall come and worship before thee, O Lord; and shall glorify thy name.

John 6:47 Verily, verily, I say unto you, he that believeth on me hath everlasting life.

Isaiah 40:12 Who hath measured the waters in the hollow of his hand, and meted out heaven with the span.

Luke 12:6 Are not five sparrows sold for two farthings, and not one of them is forgotten before God.

Psalm 100:4 Enter into his gates with thanksgiving, and into his courts with praise: be thankful unto him, and bless his name.

Entrance to Fred W. Symmes Chapel – Cleveland S.C.

Jude 25 To the only wise God our Savior, be glory and majesty, dominion and power, both now and ever. Amen.

Colossians 1:16 For by him were all things created, that are in heaven, and that are in the earth, visible and invisible.

John 3:16 For God so loved the world, that he gave his only begotten son, that whosoever believeth in him should not perish, but have everlasting life.

Matthew 5:4 Blessed are they that mourn: for they shall be comforted.

Psalm 50:10 For every beast of the forest is mine, and the cattle upon a thousand hills.

**Psalm 33:8 Let all the earth fear the Lord: let all the
inhabitants of the world stand in awe of him.**

Isaiah 1:18 Though your sins be as scarlet, they shall be as white as snow.

Psalm 46:10 Be still, and know that I am God.

Matthew 5:9 Blessed are the peacemakers: for they shall be called the children of God.

Deuteronomy 4:24 For the Lord thy God is a consuming fire, even a jealous God.

Isaiah 55:6 Seek ye the Lord while he may be found, call ye upon him while he is near.

Matthew 17:20 And Jesus said unto them, If ye have faith as a grain of mustard seed, ye shall say unto this mountain, Remove hence to younder place; and it shall remove.

Psalm 150:6 Let every thing that hath breath praise the Lord. Praise ye the Lord.

John 8:12 I am the light of the world: he that followeth me shall not walk in darkness, but shall have the light of life.

Matthew 5:45 For he maketh his sun to rise on the evil and on the good, and sendeth the rain on the just and unjust.

Matthew 6:26 Behold the fowls of the air: for they sow not, neither do they reap, nor gather into barns: yet your heavenly father feedeth them. Are ye not much better than they?

Phillipians 1:11 Being filled with the fruits of righteousness, which are by Jesus Christ, unto the glory and praise of God.

Psalm 16:11 Thou wilt shew
me the path of life: in thy
presence is fulness of joy;
at thy right hand there are
pleasures for evermore.

Psalm 136:26 O give thanks unto the God of heaven: for his mercy endureth for ever.

Psalm 103:15 As for man, his days are as grass: as a flower of the field, so he flourisheth.

Psalm 91:4 He shall cover thee with his feathers, and under his wings shalt thou trust: his truth shall be thy shield and buckler.

Matthew 11:28 Come unto me, all ye that labour and are heavy laden, and I will give you rest.

Hebrews 13:5 For he hath said, I will never leave thee, nor forsake thee.

Matthew 6:28 Consider the lilies of the field, how they grow; they toil not neither do they spin.

John 14:27 Peace I leave with you, my peace I give unto you: not as the world giveth, give I unto you.

John 3:17 For God sent not his son into the world to condem the world; but that the world through him might be saved.

John 1:3 All things were made by him; and without him was not anything made that was made.

Ephesians 2:8 For by grace are you saved through faith; and that not of yourselves: it is the gift of God.

Psalm 36:5 Thy mercy, O Lord, is in the heavens; and thy faithfulness reacheth unto the clouds.

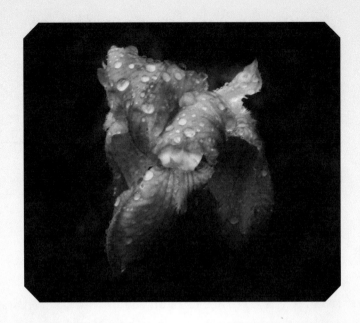

John 11:25 Jesus said unto her, I am the resurrection, and the life: he that believeth in me, though he were dead, yet shall he live.

Psalm 23:2 He maketh me to lie down in green pastures: he leadeth me beside the still waters.

Matthew 5:3 Blessed are the poor in spirit: for theirs is the kingdom of heaven.

Matthew 5:8 Blessed are the pure in heart, for they shall see God.

John 3:3 Jesus answered and said unto him, Verily, verily, I say unto thee, Except a man be born again, he cannot see the kingdom of God.

Psalm 103:12 As far as the east is from the west, so far hath he removed our transgressions from us.

Matthew 6:20 But lay up for yourselves treasures in heaven, where neither moth nor rust doth corrupt, and where thieves do not break through nor steal.

Psalm 23:4 Yea, though I walk through the valley of the shadow of death, I will fear no evil: for thou art with me.

Isaiah 43:2 When thou walkest through the fire, thou shalt not be burned; neither shall the flame kindle upon thee.

Philippines 2:10 That at the name of Jesus every knee should bow, of things in heaven, and things in earth, and things under the earth.

Hebrews 11:1 Now faith is the substance of things hoped for, the evidence of things not seen.

Colossians 3:2 Set your affection on things above, not on things on the earth.

Luke 15:6 Rejoice with me; for I have found my sheep which was lost.

1 John 4:7 Beloved, let us love one another: for love is of God; and every one that loveth is born of God, and knoweth God.

Matthew 4:19 And he saith unto them, Follow me, and I will make you fishers of men.

Exodus 33:14 And he said, my presence shall go with thee, and I will give thee rest.

Psalm 86:10 For thou art great, and doest wondrous things: thou are God alone.

John 14:3 And if I go and prepare a place for you, I will come again, and receive you unto myself; that where I am, there you may be also.

Psalm 147:8 Who covereth the heaven with clouds, who prepareth rain for the earth, who maketh grass to grow upon the mountains.

John 12:46 I am come a light into the world, that whosoever
believeth on me should not abide in darkness.

Psalm 30:5 For his anger endureth but a moment; in his favor is life: weeping may endure for a night, but joy cometh in the morning.

Ephesians 5:16 Redeeming the time, because the days are evil.

Matthew 7:7 Ask, and it shall be given you; seek, and ye shall find; knock, and it shall be opened unto you.

Matthew 7:14 Because strait is the gate, and narrow is the way, which leadeth unto life, and few there be that find it.

Matthew 25:13 Watch therefore, for ye know neither the day nor the hour wherein the Son of man cometh.

Matthew 18:20 For where two or three are gathered together in my name, there am I in the midst of them.

2 Chronicles 7:14 If my people, which are called by my name, shall humble themselves, and pray, and seek my face, and turn from their wicked ways; then will I hear from heaven, and will forgive their sin, and heal their land.

Revelation 22:13 I am Alpha and Omega, the Beginning and the End, the First and the Last.

Printed in the United States
by Baker & Taylor Publisher Services